Tonic sol -fa

W0007325

John Curwen

Alpha Editions

This edition published in 2019

ISBN : 9789389465105

Design and Setting By
Alpha Editions
email - alphaedis@gmail.com

This book is a reproduction of an important historical work. Alpha Editions uses the best technology to reproduce historical work in the same manner it was first published to preserve its original nature. Any marks or number seen are left intentionally to preserve its true form.

TWELFTH THOUSAND.

NOVELLO, EWER AND CO.'S MUSIC PRIMERS.
EDITED BY SIR JOHN STAINER.

TONIC SOL-FA

BY

JOHN CURWEN.

PRICE ONE SHILLING.
In Paper Boards, One Shilling and Sixpence.

65ᵈ

LONDON & NEW YORK
NOVELLO, EWER AND CO.

LONDON :
NOVELLO, EWER AND CO.,
PRINTERS.

PREFACE.

———•—•———

THIS Work is not intended to teach those ignorant of music how to sing, but to explain the Tonic Sol-fa Notation and method of teaching to those who are already familiar with the established mode of writing music by means of the Staff. A knowledge of that notation is taken for granted, and it will be mainly by comparing the two notations that the various points of the new notation will be made clear.

CONTENTS.

A TONIC SOL-FA PRIMER.

CHAPTER I.

RELATIONS OF THE TWO NOTATIONS.

It is often forgotten that the Staff Notation is a notation of the keyboard of the pianoforte. In the early stages of its development, when clefs were placed on any line, and the composer used as many lines—from one to twelve—as were necessary for his music, it was more of a notation of relative than of absolute pitch. But the improvement and wide diffusion of keyboard instruments has caused the notation to settle down into a pictorial representation of black and white digitals. The normal key is assumed to be C, and all other keys are represented as departures from that.

A little reflection will show that although this arrangement represents a fact of the keyboard, it has no counterpart in the experience of singers. Let us suppose that an organist finds the following chant in F too high for his choir:—

He thinks he would like to transpose it a semitone lower. With the music in F before his eyes, the following represents the process that goes on in his mind as he plays in E :—

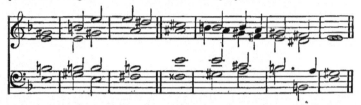

Some, perhaps, may object to this as a caricature, and say that only mechanical players transpose in this way, while all who have any ear for the inner spirit of music transpose by mentally regarding each note as the first, fifth, seventh, &c., of the key. No doubt this is true. But we are now considering the Staff Notation merely as a picture of the keyboard, and if players choose to see beyond that picture into key-relationship it is another matter, although doing so brings them very near to the Tonic Sol-fa system. By whatever mental process transposition at sight from the Staff Notation is accomplished, it gives trouble to the player. But what is the case with the singer? To him all keys are alike. The key of C is no more commonly used than F or D, and in point of convenience it is no more natural or easy than B. The process which the choir undergo in the case we have imagined is very different to that which the organist experiences. When he lowers the chant a semitone, few if any of the singers will notice it; they have no altered relationships of fingering or perpetual contradiction of signs, and they sing on as easily as before.

The fact that to singers one key is the same as another is the basis of the Tonic Sol-fa Notation. In this notation the above chant in key F appears as follows :—

KEY **F.**

m :—	s :d'	d' :t	l :—	s :s.f	m :r	d :—
d :—	d :m	f :—	fe :—	s.f:m.r	d :t,	d :—
s :—	s :s	s :—	d' :—	d' :l	s :-.f	m :—
d :—	m :d	r :—	re :—	m :f	s :s,	d :—

When transposed into key E it appears as follows :—

KEY **E.**

m :—	s :d'	d' :t	l :—	s :s.f	m :r	d :—
d :—	d :m	f :—	fe :—	s.f:m.r	d :t,	d :—
s :—	s :s	s :—	d' :—	d' :l	s :-.f	m :—
d :—	m :d	r :—	re :—	m :f	s :s,	d :—

The only difference being that the words " key E " are placed at the beginning, for the singer's guidance, instead of " key F."*

It is asserted by some that singers strike their notes by measuring the distance from one to the other—a second, a sixth, a diminished seventh, an octave, &c., without regard to the key. This being so, they say that the Staff Notation in supplying this information gives the singer all that he needs. The singer, they say, should not be perplexed with the relationship of the tones, which in modern music often changes rapidly ; all he has to do is to move along by remarking at a glance the number of semitones from the note he is on to the next. It may be true that here and there an exceptional singer possesses this power, but it is certainly not possessed by the generality of chorus-singers. To keep in mind the key-relationship of the tones is not only the easiest method, but it is the most intelligent, because it is the composer's method.†

---

* The reader is referred to the following chapters for an explanation of the signs of the notation.

† Chapter IX., or " The Mental Process in Singing," shows what are the common habits of chorus-singers in this respect.

CHAPTER II.

THE DIATONIC SCALE.

THE Tonic Sol-fa Notation consists of the initial letters of the *Sol-fa* syllables, *do* always representing the key-note. The initials of *sol* and *si* being the same, *si* is altered to *ti*. When the names are written in full they are spelled phonetically, and *sol* is invariably pronounced *soh*, that sound being more open.

Italian Names.	Written.	Noted.
si	te	t
la	lah	l
sol	soh	s
fa	fah	f
mi	me	m
re	ray	r
do	doh	d

The application of the names will be evident from the following tune :—

The upper octaves are represented by figures above the scale-letters, as $d^1 d^2$; the lower octaves by figures below, $d_1 d_2$. In *speaking* of octaves, d^1 is called "one-doh;" d_1 is called "doh-one;" and so on. In the preceding tune there are two cases of d^1. The octave commencing on middle C

is taken as a standard. The notes of that octave bear no mark above or below, and every *doh* chosen as a key-note within that octave is unmarked also. Thus these passages, so nearly alike in pitch, will have different octave marks—

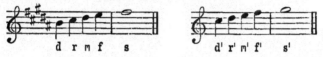

because in the first case the *doh* is within the standard octave; in the second it is above it. The tenor and bass parts are written an octave higher than they sound. Thus the passage—

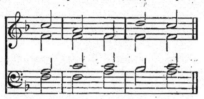

is written :—

KEY **F**.

s	m	d	l	s		s	m	d	l	s
d	d	d.	d	d		d	d	d	d	d
m	s	s	f	s	not	m̧	ş	ş	f̧	ş
d	d	m	f	m		ḑ	ḑ	m̧	f̧	m̧

It is obvious that this saves a very large number of octave marks, while it causes no practical inconvenience to the singer.

The signs of expression, such as ⎯⎯, *f*, *pp*, *cres.*, &c., are used in the Tonic Sol-fa as in the Staff Notation, as well as the Italian or English phrases which describe the style of performance. Horizontal lines are placed under the letters to express *legato*, or to tie together several notes that are to be sung to one syllable, like slurs in the Staff Notation.

CHAPTER III.

TIME.

In order to explain the Tonic Sol-fa Notation of Time it is necessary to remind the reader of the nature of musical rhythm. Music is divided by bars into measures. It is convenient, as the French do, to use the word measure to indicate the distance from one bar to the next, and to reserve the word bar for the vertical line which separates measures. This line is used in the Tonic Sol-fa Notation to mark the *commencement* of every measure, but it is not used at the end of scores as in the Staff Notation. The double bar marks the conclusion of sections or movements :—

KEY D.

d	m	s	d	f	l	l	s
d	d	r	d	d	f	f	m
m	s	s	m	f	d¹	d¹	d¹
d	d	t,	d	l,	f,	d	d

In the above example the pulses (or beats) of the music follow each other in the order of strong and weak, or accented and unaccented. The second note has a weak accent, and the sign

(6)

for this is a colon (:). The passage is therefore written as
follows :—

$$\left\{ \begin{array}{cccc}
\text{d :m} & \text{s :d} & \text{f :l} & \text{l :s} \\
\text{d :d} & \text{r :d} & \text{d :f} & \text{f :m} \\
\text{m :s} & \text{s :m} & \text{f :d'} & \text{d' :d'} \\
\text{d :d} & \text{t, :d} & \text{l, :f,} & \text{d :d}
\end{array} \right\|$$

In triple measure, where the pulses are in the order of strong,
weak, weak, the notation is as follows :—

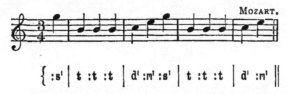

$$\left\{ \; \text{:s'} \; | \; \text{t :t :t} \; | \; \text{d' :m' :s'} \; | \; \text{t :t :t} \; | \; \text{d' :m'} \right\|$$

It will be seen from the foregoing examples that in the Tonic
Sol-fa Notation the music is cut up by the accent marks into
pulses or beats, and thus when it is desired to prolong a note
beyond one pulse we have only to place a dash through as many
pulses as we wish to hold it. So also when there is a rest no
sign is required. It is enough that the space between the two
accent marks is empty :—

Sing,   sing,   sing,   O ye heav'ns.

KEY C.

$$\left\{ \begin{array}{cccccc}
\text{d' :— :—} & \text{m' :— :} & \text{s' :— :} & \text{:d' :t} & \text{d' :} & : \\
\text{m :— :—} & \text{s :— :} & \text{s :— :} & \text{:s :f} & \text{s :} & : \\
\text{s :— :—} & \text{m' :— .} & \text{m' :— :} & \text{:m' :r'} & \text{m' :} & : \\
\text{d :— :—} & \text{d' :— :} & \text{d' :— :} & \text{:d' :r'} & \text{d' :} & :
\end{array} \right\|$$

The measures we have described contain two and three beats.
In the middle of measures which contain four or six beats there
is a subordinate accent which is expressed in the Tonic Sol-fa

Notation by a short upright line. It is called a medium accent :—

R. REDHEAD.

KEY E♭.

```
┌ s  :l │ l  :s │f  :m │ m  :r  ║
│ d  :d │-d --:d │r  :d │ d  :t, │
│ m  :f │ f  :m │s  :s │ s  :s  ║
│ d  :f,│ d  :d │t, :d │ s,  :f  ║
```

MENDELSSOHN.

How love - ly are the mes-sen-gers that preach us the gospel of peace.

KEY G.

```
{ :s,│d :- :t,│l,:- :s,│f :- :m │r :- :d │t, :d :r │s,:s, :s,│s,:-:-:-║
```

Measures are named according to the number of pulses they contain. Thus: two-pulse measure, three-pulse measure, &c. Examples of other measures are given below :—

MENDELSSOHN.

KEY A.

```
{ :s, │ s, :m  :d │ t, :- :- │ l, :- :l, │ l, :f :r │ t, :- :- │- :- ║
```

HANDEL. " Pastoral Symphony."

KEY C.

```
{│ d' :- :r' │ m' :- :f' │ s' :- :- │ l' :- :- │ s' :- :- ║
```

In the Staff Notation the same piece may be written in $\frac{3}{4}$, $\frac{3}{8}$, or even $\frac{3}{2}$ time, at the fancy of the composer. It is clear that no such variation is possible in the Tonic Sol-fa. The pulse, or beat, is the unit, and the metronome mark indicates sufficiently the speed. In marking the speed of a piece by the metronome there is no need to say ♪ = 60, ♩ = 40, &c. The pulse being always the basis of measurement, it is enough to say M. (or metronome) 60, 96, &c.

A pulse is divided into halves by placing a full stop in the middle of it; into quarters by placing a comma in the middle of each half; and into thirds by the use of two inverted commas. The following examples explain this :—

"Rule Britannia."

KEY B♭.

{ .s₁ | d   :d |d ,r .m ,f :s   .d |r   :r   .m ,f |m ||·

A sound is continued through any portion of a pulse by a continuation mark or dash, and a part-pulse silence is shown by a vacancy. The only exception to this rule is in the common time-form of a dotted crotchet followed by a quaver, or a dotted quaver followed by a semiquaver. Here the pulse divisions, being placed close together, are a sign that the sound is continued :—

HANDEL.

KEY F. Lah is D.

{ |1   :m   ,m |d   : | .d :r   .m |1₁   :— ||

ROSSINI.

KEY A♭.

{ |m   :— |— .t₁ ,d :r .t₁ .m |d   :— |1₁ . ||

Each measure being divided into pulses, any contradiction of the natural accent by syncopation is clearly shown :—

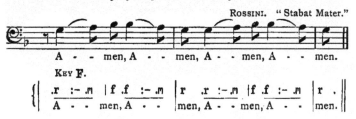

ROSSINI. "Stabat Mater."

A - - men, A - - men, A - - men, A - - men.

KEY F.

{ | .r :— .m | f .f :— .m | r   .r :— .m | f .f :— .m | r . ||
  | A - - men, A - - | men, A - - men, A - - | men. ||

A very important part of the notation of Time is that, when properly printed, each pulse in the same line of music occupies an *equal lateral space*. In the Staff Notation this rule is not observed:—

Here the measures and pulses occupy very different space, according to the number of notes they contain. The third measure is several times longer than the second. It is found a great advantage in the Tonic Sol-fa Notation to make the measures and pulses equal:—

KEY C.

| s | :— | s | :— | s | :— | |— | :— | s .s:s .s | s | :s | s | :— | |— | :— |

The pulses are measured out, like the inches on a yard measure, and the eye rapidly values the length. An experienced Sol-faist keeps time by judging the distance between the notes, only stopping occasionally to look at the accent marks; and when through bad printing the pulses are unequal, he is completely put out.

CHAPTER IV.

CHROMATIC TONES AND TRANSITION.

THE names for sharpened and flattened notes are as follows. The ordinary Sol-fa name of the note has its vowel changed to "e" for sharps, and to "a" (pronounced "aw") for flats:—

Chromatic notes are always written in full, to distinguish them from the corresponding diatonic note. Example:—

J. BARNBY.

Sleep, my pret-ty one, sleep.

Key E.

$$\{\| \text{m} :-.\text{re}:\text{m} \quad | \text{s} :-.\text{fe}:\text{s} \quad | \text{t} :-.\text{le}:\text{t} \quad | \text{d}^\text{l} :- :- \|$$

In the cases just quoted, the chromatic notes do not change the key. It is unnecessary, however, to remind the reader that modern music is full of brief entries into related keys. For example :—

When the change of key is as short as this, the flattened or sharpened notes, as in the Staff Notation, express it :—

Key F.

$$\left\{\begin{array}{l}
:\text{s} \\
:\text{d} \\
:\text{m} \\
:\text{d}
\end{array}\right.
\begin{array}{l}
\text{d}^\text{l} \\
\text{d} \\
\text{m} \\
\text{d}
\end{array}
\begin{array}{l}
:\text{m} \\
:\text{d} \\
:\text{s} \\
:\text{ta,}
\end{array}
\left|\begin{array}{l}
\text{f} \\
\text{d} \\
\text{l} \\
\text{l,}
\end{array}\right.
\begin{array}{l}
:\text{m} \\
:\text{de} \\
:\text{m} \\
:\text{s,}
\end{array}
\left|\begin{array}{l}
\text{l} \\
\text{r} \\
\text{f} \\
\text{f,}
\end{array}\right.
\begin{array}{l}
:\text{l} \\
:\text{d} \\
:\text{fe} \\
:\text{r,}
\end{array}
\left|\begin{array}{l}
\text{s} \\
\text{t,} \\
\text{s} \\
\text{s,}
\end{array}\right.
\begin{array}{l}
:\text{f} \\
:\text{t,} \\
:\text{s} \\
:\text{s,}
\end{array}
\left|\begin{array}{l}
\text{m} \\
\text{d} \\
\text{s} \\
\text{d}
\end{array}\right.
\begin{array}{l}
.- \\
:- \\
:- \\
:-
\end{array}
\left|\begin{array}{l}
- \\
- \\
- \\
-
\end{array}\right. \|$$

It has been objected by some that this is forsaking the tonic principle. The third and fourth notes in the treble, they say, are te and doh in key B♭; the seventh and eighth are ray and doh in key C. Yet they are written me, fah, and lah, soh, respectively. Of course this is true, but it is for the singer's convenience that this is done. When the change of key is lengthened, we take one note as a double or bridge-note, through which to pass into the new key. The practical use of these bridge-notes will be understood by reference to the following hymn-tune :—

HENRY SMART.

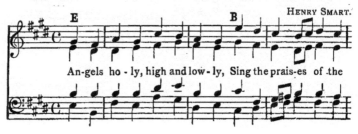

An-gels ho - ly, high and low - ly, Sing the prais-es of the

Lord! Earth and sky, all liv - ing na-ture, Man, the stamp of thy Cre-

a - tor, Praise ye, praise ye, God the Lord.

At the change to key B, the smaller and higher notes belong to the old key, the larger ones to the new. The letter "t," after B, shows that *te* is the new tone introduced by the transition; the letter "f," later on, before "E," shows that *fah* is the new tone. This is to guide the singer's ear. The change is always made at the easiest place, whether this corresponds with the exact harmonic facts or not. Thus, at the *return* to key E, the change really takes place at the middle chord of the measure; but the singers glide insensibly from the dominant seventh of key B just before into the new dominant, and hence the change is written a chord earlier. It will be seen that the sequence which occurs in this tune between the third and fourth lines of the poetry is shown in its true key-relationship by means of the bridge-tones.

CHAPTER V.

METHOD OF TEACHING.

THE previous chapters have dealt with the Tonic Sol-fa *Notation*, the mode of expressing music to the eye. We now come to the Tonic Sol-fa *method of teaching* music, the educational arrangement of facts and difficulties so as to facilitate the progress of the learner. In the elaboration of this method I have occupied the best part of my life. It is the result, gradually arrived at and even now being added to, of my own experience and the experience of many teachers of the system. Our aim has been to make the beginning and progress of the pupil easy and natural, to make his study and practice thorough and many-sided; and to give him clearness of thought by directing his attention to the real nature of music.

In the first place we teach singing *without the help of an instrument*. This is in order to give the learner independence. It is obvious that to be able to sing by hearing the notes played, or by touching them on the pianoforte, is not reading music at all; it is mere parrot-like imitation. Tonic Sol-fa singers are trained to strike their notes by the unaided judgment of their ears. This judgment is formed upon the place which each sound holds in the key, and not upon its absolute pitch or the number of semitones by which it is separated from the last note. Singers are taught to recognise a characteristic effect in each of the tones of the scale, called its mental effect. For example, in the following piece of unaccompanied recitative in Professor Macfarren's *Joseph*—

there is an incisive piercing effect produced by the seventh of the scale which no other tone would give us. It is not that it is a leap to a high note merely, for if we leap higher the effect is tamer, and if we leap lower it is tamer still :—

In the same way the characters of the other tones of the scale are brought before the learner; the boldness of the tones of the tonic chord when heard in succession, the firmness of *soh*, the calm and rest of *me*, the sadness of *lah*, the desolate sound of *fah*, and the rousing sound of *ray*.

The teacher endeavours less to *tell* the pupil the effect than to make him listen for it, and feel it for himself. The object is to fix the character of each tone in the learner's mind, so that it may be kept there, and recalled. By this means the task of sounding a given name, or naming a given sound, is made easy by the recollection which the pupil has of the *personnel* of the scale tones.

In teaching the scale a diagram called "The Modulator" is used. It enables the singer to compare modes and keys, and pass from one to another. The example opposite shows a key with its dominant (on the right side) and subdominant (on the left). A complete Modulator, embracing the whole range of keys, is given on pp. 20, 21. A large part of the pupil's first exercises are in singing voluntaries from this diagram, following with his voice the pointer of the teacher.

It is often said by casual observers that Sol-fa notes are " all on a dead level " and do not show the rise and fall of pitch as does the staff. But by early training the pictorial Modulator is fixed in the mind's eye of each pupil, and the notes start into their places in the scale as he looks at them.

We lay stress on the habit of teaching the scale gradually by means of the consonant chords which it contains. Consonance is more natural to the untrained ear than dissonance; and pure intonation is better taught by striking the tones of a chord in succession than by running up or down the scale, whose adjacent notes are dissonant with each other. First, the learner has to be made familiar with the tonic chord, *doh, me, soh,* and has to sound its tones at the will of the teacher; next he does the same with the dominant chord (*soh, te, ray*); and lastly, with the subdominant (*fah, lah, doh*). This completes the seven sounds. After this he is confined to tunes and exercises which contain no more than these seven tones, and do not change the key. Next he is introduced to the simplest form of transition—to the dominant and sub-dominant keys. Then he attacks the minor mode, chromatic notes, and distant modulations. By this gradual process of teaching his path is made easy. He learns one thing at a time, and knows that one thing thoroughly before he passes to the next. Moreover, at each step, he finds that what he has already learned helps him.

Concurrently with practice in reading from given notes, we have practice in naming given sounds. This corresponds to writing from dictation in learning a language, and this, as every one knows, is more difficult than reading. The "ear exercises," as we call them, have therefore to be kept always behind the reading exercises, but they are of great value in improving the ear.

We separate the study of Time from that of Tune. We teach it by means of the "Time Names" of M. Paris. The importance of this will be appreciated by those who have tried to teach Time to children and beginners, whether in playing or singing.

THE MODULATOR.
(COPYRIGHT.)

d'	f'	
t	m'	l
		re' ee
l	r'	s
se	de'	ba
s	DOH'	f
ba	TE	m
		le
f	ta	
m	LAH	r
la		
	ee	
r	SOH	d
	bah fe	t₁
d	FAH	
t₁	ME	l₁
	ma	
		re ee₁
l₁	RAY	s₁
se₁	de	ba
s₁	DOH	f₁
ba₁	t₁	m₁
f₁	ta₁	
m₁	l₁	r₁
	se₁	
r₁	s₁	d₁
	ba₁ fe₁	t₂
d₁	f₁	
t₂	m₁	l₂

The Time Names, slightly modified in our system, will be best seen from the following examples :—

The pupil is taught to sing his early exercises on one tone to the Time Names. Thus he first learns the Time and then the tune of a piece.. This may be considered a needless hair-splitting, but for beginners it is not so. It is found to give confidence and steadiness. The pupil becomes as certain of the rhythm of the music as he is of the sound of the notes, and enjoys slight variations of time, such as these :—

This is a brief outline of the Tonic Sol-fa method of teaching. Its chief feature is that it separates *music* from its *signs*. Music

---

* These are only a few of the simplest divisions of Time. For a complete table of Galin's Time Names the reader is referred to the Tonic Sol-fa Time Chart, or to the works of the Galin-Paris-Chevè School.

consists of sounds, and neither crotchets and quavers nor Tonic Sol-fa letters make any sound.   The Tonic Sol-fa teacher considers the ears and voices of his pupils as the material upon which he has to work.   He begins without any signs at all, and only introduces them gradually as they are needed to make the pupil recognise and recall what he knows.   This is the principle of Pestalozzi and all the educationists who have followed him.   We may sum up in a few words the Tonic Sol-fa method : to let the easy come before the difficult ; to introduce the real and concrete before the ideal or abstract ; to teach the elemental before the compound, and do one thing at a time ; to introduce both for explanation and practice the common before the uncommon ; to teach the thing before the sign, and when the thing is apprehended, attach to it a distinct sign ; to let each step, as far as possible, rise out of that which goes before, and lead up to that which comes after ; and lastly, to call in the understanding to assist the skill at every step.*

---

* See " The Teacher's Manual of the Tonic Sol-fa Method," and " Standard Course of Lessons," by John Curwen.   Tonic Sol-fa Agency, 8, Warwick Lane, E.C.

THE STUDENT'S MODULATOR.

GIVING THE STANDARD SCALE OF PITCH, WITH THE TRUE INTERVALS.

f	m		r r̃		d	t,		l,	se,
d	t,		l,	se,	s,		ba, f,	m,	
s,	ba,	f,	m,		r̄ r̃		d,	t₂	
r r̃		d	t,		l,	se, s,		ba,	f,
l,	se,	s,	ba,	f,	m,		r̄ r̃		d,
m		r r̃		d	t,		l,	se,	s,
t,		l,	se,	s,	ba,	f,	m,		r̄ r̃

♯	F	E	♯	D	♯	C	B,	♯	A,
fe / ba	**FAH**	**ME**	re / na	**RAY** r̃	de	**DOH**	t,		l,
♭	F	E	♭	D	♭	C	B,	♭	A,

	d	t,		l,	se,	s,	ba,	f,	m,
se	s,	ba,	f,	m,		r r̃		d,	t₂
	r r̃		d	t,		l,	se,	s,	ba,
	l,	se,	s,	ba,	f,	m,		r̃ r̃	
f	m		r r̃		d	t,		l,	se,
d	t,		l,	se,	s,	ba,	f,	m,	
s		ba	f	m		r		d	t,

CHAPTER VI.

METHOD OF TEACHING HARMONY.

HARMONY, whether expressed in the Staff Notation or not, is manifestly a matter of key-relationship. In discussing the merits of any progression the *pitch* of the notes is a mere accident; the right or wrong depends on their place in the key. We may correct a fault by saying "the F should descend to E," but the remark has no value beyond the particular case to which it is applied: it is not a rule or a generalisation. And though musicians commonly talk of harmony in this way, it is impossible that they should *think* of it except in relation to key. Hence the frequent use in teaching of the terms "subdominant," "leading-note," "seventh," "minor ninth," &c., all of which express that relationship of tones which is independent of their pitch. So far we must have the consent of every musician. Is it not easy to go a step farther, and perceive that the Tonic Sol-fa Notation, which is a notation of key-relationship and only by inference a notation of pitch, is specially adapted for expressing harmony? We will first explain the Tonic Sol-fa notation of harmony, and then the method of teaching the subject.

Many celebrated teachers of harmony have felt the shortcomings of the system of figured basses, in that the figures do not show the *roots* of the chords, upon which the laws of progression so largely depend. One or two (especially Gottfried Weber and Gersbach) have used for their pupils a system of chord names on the same principle as those which, after several years of inquiry and experiment, I decided to adopt for Tonic Sol-faists. The nomenclature is very simple. We call each chord of the scale by its Sol-fa initial letter, printed in capitals to distinguish it from the note of the scale. For example :—

C. E. HORSLEY.

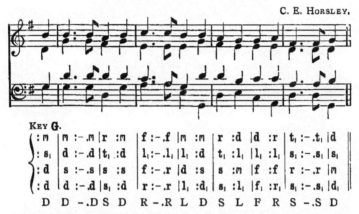

KEY **G**.

```
{ : m  | m :- .m | r :m  | f :- .f | m :m  | r :d | d :r  | t₁ :- .t₁ | d   ||
{ : s₁ | d :- .d | t₁ :d | l₁:- .l₁ | l₁ :d | t₁ :l₁ | l₁ :l₁ | s₁ :- .s₁ | s₁  ||
{ : d  | s :- .s | s :s  | f :- .r | d :s  | s :m | f :f  | r :- .r | m   ||
{ : d  | d :- .d | s₁ :d | r :- .r | l₁ :d₁ | s₁ :l₁ | f₁ :r₁ | s₁ :- .s₁ | d₁  ||

  D    D  -.D S  D      R -.R  L     D    S    L    F    R    S -.S D
```

Chords in the minor mode are expressed by italic capitals. The positions of a chord in relation to the bass are expressed by the letters *a*, *b*, *c*, &c., after its name. The direct form of the chord is its " *a* position " (the *a* is in practice omitted), the first inversion its " *b* position," and so on. A dissonant passing tone is shown by the letter *p;* a consonant passing tone by the letters *cp*. A passing tone which does not " pass," but returns to the note it starts from, is known as a " waving tone." The minor dominant is known as ^{se}*M*. The addition of a fourth, seventh, or ninth to a chord is shown by a figure at the upper left-hand side of the chord name: ⁷R, ⁴S, &c. These rules will be best understood from the following example :—

"Lutheran Choral."

KEY **C**.

```
( :m  | l  :s |f  :m | r  :— |m | t  | d' :d' |t.l:t | l :-|-,|
{ :d  | d.r:m |l₁.t₁:d | d  :t₁ |d | r  | d.r:m |m :m.r | d :-|-|
{ :l  | 1.t:d'|r' :s | l  :s |s | se | 1  :1 |1 :se | l :-|-,|
( :l .s| f  :m |r  :d | f₁ :s₁ |d | t₁ | l₁.t₁:d.r|m :m  | l₁:-|-|

  L    F :Db|R  :D|⁷Rb :S |D |SEb| L  : Lb|⁴ⁿM :⁸ᵉ⁷ᵐM| L :-|-|
  p    2p    cp            |   |2p  p   w
```

We have already shown (p. 12) that brief entries into related
keys are expressed for convenience in the old key by help of
altered notes.   But in analysing harmony by means of the chord
names the harmonic truth is always exactly given.

In the Tonic Sol-fa system a clear distinction is made between
chromatic and transitional chords, between flattened or sharpened
notes which threaten to change the key but end in re-affirming it,
and those which mark the passage into a new key.   This distinction is drawn by Professor Macfarren in his theoretical works.
For example, in the following passage we teach that there are
two transitions, first to B flat and then to C :—

On the other hand we teach that when the same melody is
harmonised as below, the flat and naturals do *not* establish a new
key, and are purely chromatic :—

This distinction, which is carried out through all the studies of
our pupils, leads them to take a broad and connected view of
music, to regard it as a series of progressions and not as isolated
chords.   We have heard such a passage as this spoken of as
ending in the relative minor :—

Great confusion exists among learners on this point. We have met with some who have a notion that the " chord of F " denotes " the key of F," and who have never heard that to establish the key of any passage we must look before and after. Tonic Sol faists are taught that no one chord can establish a key, but that to do this in the course of a piece of music requires a movement from dominant to tonic of the new key.

The method of teaching harmony trains the observation of the ear simultaneously with that of the eye. The pupil begins by *hearing* a common chord and experiencing its consonance. The chord is then taken to pieces, and the source of its sweetness is shown to be the third, and the source of its strength the fifth. A single chant in four parts, made up of tonic and dominant chords, is then heard. Afterwards the subdominant is intro-duced ; the pupil is then led to hear a dissonance, and learns that his ear feels satisfaction in its resolution, and dissatisfaction if the dissonant note leaps away. Then follows the chord of the dominant seventh and the full close which it produces when followed by the tonic. Afterwards the second inversion of the tonic chord, and then the half-close or cadence on the dominant. The essence of the system is that it teaches the commonest and most used combinations first. Instead of spreading before the pupil all the direct chords, all the first inversions, sevenths on every chord, &c., it picks out the commonplaces of simple music, and teaches them first, introducing dissonances, less used inver-sions, &c., one by one in the order of their frequency. For a student who is familiar with harmony it may be profitable to compile a classified table of consonances, dissonances, &c., which the eye can cover. For purposes of recapitulation such a table is very useful. But we maintain that it is not the natural order for the learner. To give the pupil one tool at a time, and teach him the use of that before giving him another, has ever been the method of educationists. The study of composition is carried on concurrently with that of chords. There are three forms of exercises—first, filling in the inner parts when the air and bass and names of the chords are given (this is the easiest) ; second, writing upon a figured or rather lettered bass ; and, third, har-monising a given melody with the instruction to introduce certain chords, but leaving the pupil to find out the way. By means of the post, composition is now being taught on this system to hundreds of students in Great Britain, the Colonies, India, &c.

CHAPTER VII.

THOSE who have been trained upon the Established Notation of music will naturally inquire what are the relationships of the Tonic Sol-fa to the older Notation ? Is the new Notation intended to supersede the old, and what do Tonic Sol-faists do when they want to learn the Staff Notation?

There is no rivalry between the two systems. Prejudice still lingers here and there, but musical men are fast coming to see that music is a thing which lies behind all systems and notations, and that this or that system is to be valued according as it teaches music thoroughly and well. We need not trouble ourselves with any idea of disestablishing the Staff Notation. Apart from its merits, its mere establishment is an argument for its preservation, and a sort of argument which has especial weight with Englishmen. No Tonic Sol-fa teacher is ever so foolish as to try to prejudice his pupils against the Staff Notation. We strongly disapprove, for educational reasons, of its being introduced until the learner has mastered the facts of music— Time, Tune, Modulation, the Minor Mode, &c., from our Notation, but the best of our pupils are always eager to pass on to the Staff Notation when the proper time arrives. The introduction of the Staff Notation is postponed merely that the pupil's progress may be the sounder in the end, and not from any desire to keep it from him. Let us suppose a pupil who is able to sing at sight from Tonic Sol-fa such music as a Handel chorus of moderate difficulty, wanting to learn the Staff Notation. It has often been asserted that our system leaves our pupils high and dry when they have learnt it, and shuts them off from the universal language of the art. But a pupil of this sort has very little to learn. His voice obeys his ear, his eye reports to his mind the notes of the printed page, he knows how to use his voice and to sing in tune. What he has to learn are the *signs* of the Staff Notation. He is in the position of an arithmetician who wants to learn the signs of algebra, or of an English veteran who has passed into a foreign army and has to pick up the new words of command. All that he has learned is of use ; what he has to do is to adapt himself to a new nomenclature and symbolism.

But there is no need to construct a supposed case, for we can in this matter appeal to experience. Every year we are turning out readers of the Staff Notation by the thousand, and the testimony of choirmasters all over the country is that Sol-faists make the best readers. The intermediate Sol-fa certificate can be taken with or without passing a test in singing at sight from the Staff Notation. But it is found that two-thirds of the many who have taken this certificate have elected to attempt the Staff Notation test, and have passed it. In the higher certificates the Staff Notation is still optional, but the proportion who pass in it is so great that it is the exception to omit it. When harmony and composition has been learned on our system it is in the same way quite easy to express one's knowledge in the Staff Notation. No one will suspect Mr. Hullah's examination in the Theory of Music, under the Society of Arts, to be in any degree tainted with Tonic Sol-faism, but close upon two-thirds of those who have passed it during the last ten years have been Tonic Sol-faists. In the still higher departments of knowledge we may refer to those gentlemen who have recently proceeded Mus. Bac. at Cambridge, who are Sol-faists. They think out their harmony in the Tonic Sol-fa letters, and make a rough copy of their exercises in the New Notation.

As, therefore, it is only *signs* that the practised Sol-faist has to learn in passing to the Staff Notation, we teach him the signs by *writing*. The best way to learn the characters of a new alphabet is by writing them, and so we give him graduated exercises in writing from Tonic Sol-fa Notation into Staff Notation, and *vice-versâ*. When he has the signs at command he can proceed to sight-reading from the Staff Notation to his heart's content, and when he has arrived at this point he is considered capable of looking after himself. In practice the Tonic Sol-fa Notation is concurrent with the Staff Notation, and helpful to it, not antagonistic.

CHAPTER VIII.

THE MINOR MODE.

WE regard the minor mode as historically developed from the old Greek and church mode on the sixth of the major scale, whose notes are the unaltered intervals of the relative major. We teach our pupils that the sharpened seventh has come in with the growth of harmony, in order to make a satisfactory dominant chord. In its original unaltered form the natural seventh is still used as a passing note, and as the note of a chord when the bass moves down by step. The sharpened sixth (which note we call *bah*) follows naturally from the alteration of the leading note, and was intended to avoid the augmented second in passing to or from the leading note. But the sixth is still used in its natural form, producing, when followed by the leading note, a pathetic effect in melody, and forming an essential part of the subdominant chord in a full close. We deny that the minor mode has any title to be considered a *key* in the same way as the major, first, because of the variableness of its scale ; second, because its chief practical use in common music is as an appendage to its relative major. A composition strictly in the minor from beginning to end is very rarely to be met with. There is a constant passing to the relative major as the stronger key.

To a Tonic Sol-faist, therefore, the minor mode is the " *lah* mode." He has been already taught that the sixth of the major scale has a mental effect of sadness, and this effect is heightened by its being lifted to the importance of a tonic. It is explained that for purposes of *harmony* the seventh from *lah* is generally sharpened, and for purposes of *melody* the sixth from *lah* is sometimes sharpened. Thus the minor mode flows easily out of the relative major. A minor passage is named from the key of

(28)

its relative major, with the additional words, "lah is C, G, F♯,"
&c., as the case may be. The following is an example:—

The Staff Notation, itself an historical growth, supports this
view by giving the same signature to a key and its relative minor.
Here is a passage, for example, which is strictly in the key of C
minor. We give the Tonic Sol-fa interpretation at the side:—

The only altered note here is the B, and this exactly corresponds
with the Tonic Sol-fa Notation, in which the only altered note is
se. If, however, with some modern theorists we regard C major
and C minor as one and the same key, the minor scale being a
mere modification of the *tonic* major, we should have to write the
passage in both notations as follows :—

Here instead of one altered note there are eight. It has been
suggested by several critics that we should write minor music in

c

this way, treating the third, minor sixth, and minor seventh as accidentals, and the sharp sixth and seventh as diatonic notes. But, as a fact, no teachers have ever attempted to Sol-fa the minor mode as if it were an alteration of the tonic major, and the theorists who have urged us to do so are not themselves in the habit of Sol-faing, and are not sensible of the difficulties it would involve. It would in fact be easier to adopt the modern Italian method of the fixed *do*, and easier still to give up Sol-faing altogether, than to adopt this proposal. The old English practice (see Webbe's Solfeggios) was to call the key-note of the minor mode *lah*, and this plan is pursued wherever in England and America and France Sol-faing with the movable *do* is practised from the Staff Notation.

The difference between us and the theorists we have referred to is, however, a surface one. There is no disagreement about the rules of harmonising minor passages, no question as to the beauty of the minor mode. We cannot be charged with confusing the major with the minor, for appealing to results we find our singers more confident in minor music, and our harmony students as correct in their use of the two scales and in their discrimination between them as average learners on the other system. Some writers go so far as to object to the term " relative minor " altogether, and speak of it as delusive and false. Whatever language we use, however, we must all agree that in major music the minor key of the sixth is entered at least three times as often as the minor key of the first, and conversely in minor music the major key of the third at least three times as often as the major key of the first. Whether, in view of these habits of music, the word " relative " may be fairly applied to one scale more than the other, we leave common-sense to decide. In the Tonic Sol-fa method a distinction is made between modulation and transition. Modulation is used in its old sense of change of mode, and transition for change of key.

CHAPTER IX.

THE MENTAL PROCESS IN SINGING.

THAT singers do not produce their notes by passing mechanically from interval to interval, but that their ears are constantly remembering and expecting the tonal relationship of the harmony, is proved by the *mistakes* in classical oratorios, &c., which may commonly be heard in undertrained choirs. We give a few cases, all of which we have ourselves heard and noted in performances of more or less celebrated choirs.

In the chorus " Glory to God," from Handel's *Joshua*, the music, though in the signature of D, comes to a decided close in G and then returns suddenly to D :—

Thunders, heav'n thunders, tempests roar, and groans the ground.

The C sharp in the bass, at the word " groans," which announces the return to D, is approached by a wide leap, and a number of the voices sing C natural. In the Tonic Sol-fa Notation attention is called to this new note by the change of key, and the sense of " mental effect " which the singers possess would not allow them to sing the piercing " te " as a " fah ":—

KEY G.   D.t.

s	.m	:s		d'	.s	:s	.s	s :	·¹ r'		r' :- .r'	t

Thunders,heav'n thunders, tempests roar, and groans the ground.

| m | .d | :d | | m | .m | :m | „r | m : | ·d f | | f :- .f | m |

| d' | .s | :s | | d' | .d' | :d' | „t | d' : | ·m l | | r' :- .t | r' |

Thunders,heav'n thunders, tempests roar, and groans the ground.

| d | .d, | :d | | d | .d | :m | .s | d : | ·¹ ,r | | t :- .l | se |

(31)

The following passage from "He sent a thick darkness"
(*Israel*) is an example of the confusion of major and minor :—

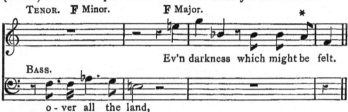

The first phrase is in F minor, and the tenors in taking up the
second phrase remain in F minor and sing the A that is marked
with an asterisk *flat* instead of natural. The Tonic Sol-faist
associates " syllable with interval," and would never sing a whole
tone between *fah* and *me* at this place :—

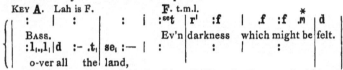

In the chorus "And with the blast" (*Israel*), the music (though
in the signature of D) has been for ten or more bars in G, and a
change to A involves a C sharp in the tenor, which is sung
natural :—

In Tonic Sol-fa :—

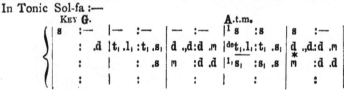

Here the change of notation calls attention to the new note.

The following passage from Mendelssohn's *St. Paul* is often wrongly sung at the place marked. The tenor and bass parts are given as sufficient for illustration :—

The music, as the accompaniment clearly shows, changes unexpectedly to F major and the E becomes natural. But it is often sung flat.

In the chorus " He trusted in God " (*Messiah*) there is a passage in which the fall of a minor and a major third is alternated :—

It is quite common in amateur performances of the oratorio to hear a confusion of tone at the points marked with an asterisk. This error is not caused by change of key, but apparently by the failure of the Staff Notation to force the singers to remember at what part of the scale they are, and where the semitones come. In Tonic Sol-fa Notation the use of a name for each scale-tone helps the singers to fix its place :—

These quotations are sufficient to prove the point that the majority of singers, whatever theories they may hold as to the mental process by which they produce their tones, do really as a fact depend upon key-relationship, and that when this relationship is abruptly disturbed or momentarily uncertain they betray their mental habits by keeping to the old key.

We give two examples of remote changes of key during the course of a movement, which appear fictitiously complex in the Staff Notation through the crowd of necessary accidentals. The more simple Tonic Sol-fa version is given under each :—

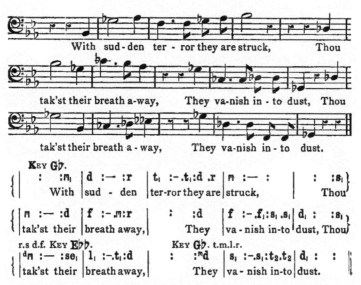

In these cases the complexity is *not* in the music itself. The composer has not thought it worth while to change the signature, and the passage becomes a puzzle to ordinary eyes through being written in a distant key, which requires a crowd of signs and countersigns to adjust the staff relationship of the notes. In the Tonic Sol-fa Notation the key is in all cases directly stated, and the most remote transition becomes clear. Examples of this sort might easily have been multiplied from standard works.

PRACTICAL EXERCISES.

THE plan which we adopt for teaching the Staff Notation to Tonic Sol-faists, will be here adopted for teaching the Tonic Sol-fa Notation to those familiar with the Staff, namely, a series of graded exercises in converting music from one notation into the other. The easier process of translating from the unfamiliar into the familiar (from Tonic Sol-fa into Staff) is placed first; then the converse process of translating from Staff into Tonic Sol-fa.

CHAPTER II.

TRANSLATE into Staff Notation, treble clef, a crotchet to every note :—

I.
KEY E♭.   German Choral.

{|s |s d' |t :l |s f |ᴍ ᴍ |r d |f r |ᴍ ᴍ |r s }

{||s d' |t l |s f |ᴍ r |r ᴍ |f ᴍ |r r |d ||

2.
KEY F.   Rev. Sir F. A. GORE OUSELEY.

{|d d r |t, t, d r |ᴍ s f r |ᴍ d t, l, }

{||s, t, d r |ᴍ d f s |l l s f |ᴍ s d r |d ||

Translate into Staff Notation, bass clef, a minim to every note :—

3.
KEY A.   Bass of Hymn-tune "Norfolk."

{|d, |d t, d l, |s, f, ᴍ, s, |d d, t₂ d, |r, r, s, f, }

{||s, ᴍ, f, s, |ᴍ r d t, |l, s, f, ᴍ, |r. s, d, ||

Translate into Staff Notation, in vocal score, a crotchet to every note :—

4.
Key E.   H. J. GAUNTLETT.

m	m f s d'	t l s s	m f r d	r r m ‖
d	d d d m	r f m r	d d t, d	d t, d
s	s f m s	s t d' s	s l s m	l s s
d	d r m d	s r m t,	d f, s, l,	f, s, d

Translate into Tonic Sol-fa Notation, using no other accent marks than the bar :—

5.

6.   Bass of Hymn-tune by HENRY SMART.

7.   R. REDHEAD.

8.   R. REDHEAD.

9.   Bass of German Choral.

CHAPTER III.

TRANSLATE into Staff Notation, treble clef, a crotchet to a pulse :—

10.
Key G.   HANDEL. "Samson."

| m :s :r | m :— : | : :t | d' :— :— ‖ |

Translate into Staff Notation, treble clef, a minim **to a** pulse :—

11.

KEY C.　　　　　　　　　　　　　　　　　　Dr. GAUNTLETT.

{|m :d | s :m |l :l | s :— |m' :r' | d' :t |l :d' | d' :—|s :— ||

{|d' :s | l :m | s :f | m :— |m' :t | d' :s |l :d' | r' :—|d' :— ||

Translate into Staff Notation, treble clef, a quaver to a pulse :—

12.

KEY A.　　　　　　　　　　　G. A. MACFARREN. " Joseph."

{:s₁ | s :— :m |d :— :s₁| d :— :— |l₁:— : | d :— :— |f :— :m | m :— :— |— :— ||

Translate into Staff Notation, treble clef, a quaver to a pulse :—

13.

KEY C.　　　　　　　G. A. MACFARREN. " The Lady of the Lake."

{:d' | s' ·f' :m' |m' :r' :d' |d' :t :l | s :— :— |— :— : | : :s }

{| d' :— :— |— :— :d' |d' :— :d' | m' :— :d' |s :— : | : ||

Translate into Staff Notation, treble clef, a quaver to a pulse :—

14.

KEY G.　　　　　　　　　　　　　　HANDEL. " Samson."

{| d ,m :s :s | s :f ,m :r ,d | t₁,r :f :m | r :— :— ||

Translate into Staff Notation, treble clef, a crotchet to a pulse :—

15.

KEY G.　　　　　　　　　　　　　　HANDEL. " Samson."

{| .s :d .r |m ,r ,m ,f:m ,f .r ,m | d .r :m .f |s ,f .s ,l:s ,l ,f ,s}

{| m ,s :d' .t |d .s,f :m .r ,d | s ||

16.

KEY C.　　　　　　　　　　　　MENDELSSOHN. " Elijah."

{| d :— .m |s ,,s :d' ,,d' | r' :— |r' .t :s ,f,f| m :m ||

17.

KEY C.   HAYDN. "Creation."

$\left\{\left\|\ r^l.m^l:f^l\ .s^l\left|l^l\ .m^l:f^l\ .r^l\right|\ d^l.r^l.d^l:m^l.f^l.m^l\left|d^l.r^l.d^l:m^l.f^l.m^l\right|\ s^l\ :-\ |-\ :-\ \right\|\right.$

18.

KEY F.   HAYDN. "Creation."

$\left\{\left\|\ m\ :f\ :r\ \left|d\ .m:-\ .s:-\ .t\right|\ -.d^l:-\ .t:l\ .s\ \left|f\ :-,s.n,f:r,m.d,r\right\}\right.\right.$

$\left\{\left\|\ t_l\ :\ .r,m:s,f.m,r\left|d\ :-\ :-\ \right\|\right.\right.$

Translate the following passages into Tonic Sol-fa Notation :—

19.   DR. BOYCE.

20.   TESCHNER.

21.   TESCHNER.

22.   E. PROUT.

23.   MENDELSSOHN.

24.   DR. CROFT.

25.   MOZART.

CHAPTER IV.

TRANSLATE into Staff Notation, a crotchet to a pulse :—

32.
KEY **D.**   HENRY SMART.

: d¹	t	:l	se	:s	fe	:f	m	:—	—	:r	d
: m	f	:fe	m	:—	—	:r	d	:—	t,	:—	d
: m¹	r¹	:d¹	t	:ta	l	:la	s	:—	f	:—	m
: d	r	:re	m	:de	r	:f	s,	:—	s,	:—	d

Translate into Tonic Sol-fa Notation :—

33.   ROSSINI.

34.   G. A. MACFARREN.   Chromatic Sentences.

Translate into Staff Notation, treble clef, a minim to a
pulse :—

35.
KEY **G.**   B. LAMB.

| { | d | :— | m | :fe | s | :— | ‖ s | :— | l | :s | r | :r | d | :— | ‖ |

36.
KEY **G.**   Dr. W. CROTCH.

| { | m | :— | l | :fe | s | :— | ‖ r | :— | f | :m | r | :r | d | :— | ‖ |
| { | d | :— | d | :r | t, | :— | ‖ ta, | :— | l,.t,:d | | d | :t, | d | :— | ‖ |

Translate into Tonic Sol-fa Notation, by the use of chromatic notes :—

Translate into Staff Notation, keeping the signature of E throughout :—

39.   J. BARNBY.

KEY **E**.   r.s.d.f. **C**.   **B** t.m.l.r.s.

d .l :s	:m .s	$d^l m^l$:– .m^l :r^l .,r^l	d^l	:d^l	:^{t}d .d
d .fe₁:s₁	:	^{ma}s :– .s :f .,f	m	:m^i	:^{a} la₁.la₁
m .re :m	:	$d^l m^l$:– .m^l :t .,t	d^l	:d^l	:$^{m^l}$f .f
d :d	:	$^{la}d^l$:– .d^l :s .,s	l	:l	:^{t}d .d

t₁	:– .t₁ :t₁ .t₁	d	:–
s₁	:– .s₁ :s₁ .s₁	s₁	:–
f	:– .f :f .f	m	:–
r	:– .s₁ :s₁ .s₁	d	:–

Translate into Tonic Sol-fa Notation, showing the transitions by the use of bridge-notes :—

CHAPTER V.

41. WRITE the Time-names of Exercise 29.

42. Write the Time-names of Exercise 31.

CHAPTER VI.

43. COPY the first four measures of the Easter Hymn, printed at the beginning of Chapter III., and write under the bass the Tonic Sol-fa Chord-names and positions.

44. Translate into Tonic Sol-fa Notation, Joule's Chant, Exercise 40, and write under the bass the Tonic Sol-fa Chord-names and positions, marking also the discords. Note that the third inversion of a discord is called the *d* position.

CHAPTER VIII.

TRANSLATE into Staff Notation, treble clef, a minim to a pulse :—

45.
KEY **F.**   J. KENT.

$$\{ \| \text{s} \ :- \ | \text{t}_\text{,} :\text{d} \ | \text{r} \ :- \ \| \text{s} \ :- \ | \text{f .m} :\text{r .d} \ \text{d} \ :\text{t}_\text{,} \ | \text{d} \ :- \ \|$$

46.
KEY **A♭**, lah is **F.**   J. KENT.

$$\{ \| \text{m} \ :- \ | \text{se}_\text{,} :\text{l}_\text{,} \ | \text{t}_\text{,} \ :- \ \| \text{m} \ :- \ | \text{r .d} :\text{t}_\text{,}.\text{l}_\text{,} | \text{l}_\text{,} \ :\text{se}_\text{,} \ | \text{l}_\text{,} \ :- \ \|$$

Translate into Staff Notation, treble clef, a crotchet to a pulse :—

47.
KEY **E♭**, lah is **C.**   S. REAY.

$$\{ :\text{1} \ | \text{m} \ :\text{r} \ | \text{d} \ :\text{t}_\text{,}.\text{l}_\text{,} | \text{m} \ :- \ | \text{r}_\text{,} \ :\text{ba} \ | \text{se} :\text{1} \ | \text{t} :\text{r}^\text{l}.\text{d} | \text{t} \ :- | - \|$$

48.
KEY **C**, lah is **A.**   HENRY SMART.

$$\{ :\text{1 .se} | \text{1} \ :\text{t} \ | \text{se}.\text{ba} :\text{se .1} | \text{t} \ :\text{se} | \text{m} \ :\text{1 .se} | \text{1} \ :\text{se} \ | \text{t} \ :\text{m} \ | \text{d}^\text{l} :- | - \|$$

Translate into Tonic Sol-fa Notation :—

49.   LA TROBE.

50.   HANDEL.

CHAPTER IX.

TRANSLATE into Staff Notation, with the signature of E flat (not C flat) throughout.

51.
Key C♭.   G. A. MACFARREN. "Joseph."

{ :t .t | d¹ :– .r¹ :m¹ | l :f¹ : .d¹ | d¹ :– .r¹ :m¹ }

{ | l :f¹ :d¹ .d¹,r¹| m¹ :— :m¹ | l :– .m¹ :d¹ .l }

f. F♭.
{ |ᵗᵃf.,f :s : | r :f :m .m | f :s :l | t :· · }

NOVELLO, EWER & CO.'S
MUSIC PRIMERS
EDITED BY
SIR JOHN STAINER.

Any of the above may be had strongly bound in boards, price 6d. each extra.

LONDON & NEW YORK: NOVELLO, EWER AND CO.
28/9/93.

ORATORIOS, CANTATAS, &c.

PRICE ONE SHILLING EACH.

Anderton, T.—THE NORMAN BARON.
—— THE WRECK OF THE HESPERUS.

Aspa, E.—THE GIPSIES.

Astorga—STABAT MATER.

Bach—GOD SO LOVED THE WORLD.
—— GOD GOETH UP WITH SHOUTING.
—— GOD'S TIME IS THE BEST.
—— MY SPIRIT WAS IN HEAVINESS.
—— O LIGHT EVERLASTING.
—— BIDE WITH US.
—— A STRONGHOLD SURE.
—— MAGNIFICAT.
—— THOU GUIDE OF ISRAEL.
—— JESU, PRICELESS TREASURE.
—— JESUS, NOW WILL WE PRAISE THEE.
—— WHEN WILL GOD RECALL MY SPIRIT.

Barnby, J.—REBEKAH.

Beethoven—THE CHORAL FANTASIA.
—— THE CHORAL SYMPHONY (the Vocal portion).
—— ENGEDI.
—— MOUNT OF OLIVES.
—— MASS, IN C (Latin Words).
——*MASS, IN C.
—— RUINS OF ATHENS.

Bendl, Karel. — WATER-SPRITE'S REVENGE (Female Voices).

Bennett, Sir W. S.—EXHIBITION ODE, 1862.

Betjemann, G. R.—THE SONG OF THE WESTERN MEN.

Blair, Hugh.—HARVEST-TIDE.

Brahms, J.—A SONG OF DESTINY.

Bridge, J. F.—*ROCK OF AGES.
—— THE INCHCAPE ROCK.
—— THE LORD'S PRAYER.

Bunnett, E.—OUT OF THE DEEP (PS. 130).

Carissimi—JEPHTHAH.

Cherubini—*REQUIEM MASS, IN C MINOR.
—— THIRD MASS, IN A (Coronation).
—— FOURTH MASS, IN C.

Costa, Sir M.—THE DREAM.

Ellicott, Rosalind F.—ELYSIUM.

Franz, Robert.—PRAISE YE THE LORD (117th Psalm).

Gade, Niels W.—ZION.
—— SPRING'S MESSAGE. 8d.
—— CHRISTMAS EVE.
—— THE ERL-KING'S DAUGHTER.

Garrett, G.—HARVEST CANTATA.

Garth, R. M.—THE WILD HUNTSMAN.

Gaul, A. R.—A SONG OF LIFE.

Gluck—ORPHEUS (Act II.)

Goetz, Hermann.—BY THE WATERS OF BABYLON.
—— NŒNIA.

Goodhart, A. M. — EARL HALDAN'S DAUGHTER.

Gounod, Ch.—DE PROFUNDIS (PS. 130).
—— DITTO (Out of Darkness).
—— MESSE SOLENNELLE (Latin Words).
—— THE SEVEN WORDS OF OUR SAVIOUR ON THE CROSS.
—— DAUGHTERS OF JERUSALEM.
——*GALLIA.

Grimm, J. O.—THE SOUL'S ASPIRATION.

Hecht, E.—O MAY I JOIN THE CHOIR INVISIBLE.

Handel.—CHANDOS TE DEUM.
—— ODE ON ST. CECILIA'S DAY.
—— THE WAYS OF ZION.
—— MESSIAH (Pocket Edition).
—— ISRAEL IN EGYPT (Ditto).
—— JUDAS MACCABÆUS (Ditto).
—— DETTINGEN TE DEUM.
—— UTRECHT JUBILATE.
—— O PRAISE THE LORD.
—— ACIS AND GALATEA.
—— ACIS AND GALATEA. Edited by J. BARNEY.
—— O COME, LET US SING UNTO THE LORD.

Haydn.—THE CREATION (Pocket Edition).
—— SPRING. SUMMER. AUTUMN. WINTER.
——*FIRST MASS, IN B FLAT.
—— FIRST MASS, IN B FLAT (Latin).
—— SECOND MASS, IN C (Latin).
—— THIRD MASS (Imperial). (Latin).
——*THIRD MASS (Imperial).
——*TE DEUM.

Hiller, Dr.—A SONG OF VICTORY.

Hofmann, H. — SONG OF THE NORNS (Female Voices).

Hummel.—First Mass, in B flat.
—— Second Mass, in E flat.
—— Third Mass, in D.

Huss, H. H.—Ave Maria (Female Voices).

Iliffe, F.—St. John the Divine.

Jensen, A.—The Feast of Adonis.

Kilburn, N.—The Lord is my Shepherd.

Leo, Leonardo.—Dixit Dominus.

Lloyd, C. Harford. — The Song of Balder.

MacCunn, H.—Lord Ullin's Daughter.

Macfarren, G. A.—Outward Bound.
—— May Day.

Mackenzie, A. C.—The Bride.

Mee, J. H.—Horatius (Male Voices).

Mendelssohn.—St. Paul (Pocket Edition).
—— Elijah (Pocket Edition).
—— Loreley.
—— Hymn of Praise.
—— As the Hart Pants.
—— Come, let us Sing.
—— When Israel out of Egypt came.
—— Not unto us.
—— Lord, how long.
—— Hear my Prayer.
—— The First Walpurgis Night.
—— Midsummer Night's Dream.
—— Man is Mortal.
—— Festgesang (Hymns of Praise).
—— Festgesang (Male Voices).
—— Christus.
—— To the Sons of Art.
——*Ave Maria (Saviour of Sinners).
——*Three Motets (Female Voices).

Meyerbeer.—91st Psalm (Latin Words).
—— 91st Psalm (English Words).

Mozart.—King Thamos.
——*First Mass.
—— Seventh Mass (Latin).
—— Twelfth Mass (Latin).
——*Twelfth Mass.
—— Requiem Mass (Latin).
——*Requiem Mass.

Mundella, E.—Victory of Song (Female Voices).

Parker, H. W.—The Kobolds.

Parry, C. H. H.—Blest Pair of Sirens.
—— The Glories of our Blood and State.

Pergolesi.—Stabat Mater (Female V.).

Pinsuti, C.—Phantoms.

Prout, E.—Freedom.
—— The Hundredth Psalm.

Purcell.—Te Deum and Jubilate, in D.

Read, J. F. H.—In the Forest (Male V.).

Romberg.—The Lay of the Bell.
—— The Transient and the Eternal.

Rossini.—*Stabat Mater.

Sach, Ed.—Water Lilies.

Sangster, W. H.—Elysium.

Schubert.—Song of Miriam.
—— Mass, in A flat.
—— Mass, in B flat.
—— Mass, in C.
—— Mass, in F.
—— Mass, in G.

Schumann.—The Pilgrimage of the Rose.
—— The King's Son.
—— Mignon's Requiem.
—— Advent Hymn, "In Lowly Guise."
—— Manfred.
—— New Year's Song.

Schutz, H.—The Passion of our Lord.

Silas, E.—Mass, in C.

Smith, Alice Mary.—The Song of the Little Baltung (Men's Voices).
—— Ode to the North-East Wind.
—— The Red King (Men's Voices).

Spohr.—The Last Judgment.
—— God, Thou art Great.
—— The Christian's Prayer.
—— Hymn to St. Cecilia.

Such, E. C.—God is our Refuge (Psalm 46).

Sullivan, A.—Exhibition Ode.
—— Festival Te Deum.

Thomas, A. Goring.—The Sun Worshippers.

Thorne, E. H.—Be Merciful unto me.

Van Bree.—St. Cecilia's Day.

Waller, Hilda.—The Singers (Female Voices).

Weber, C. M. von.—Preciosa.
——*Mass, in G.
——*Mass, in E flat.
—— Jubilee Cantata.
—— Three Seasons.

Wesley, S.—Dixit Dominus.

Wesley, S. S.—O Lord, Thou art my God.

Wood, C.—Ode to the West Wind.

The Works marked * have Latin and English Words.

LONDON AND NEW YORK: NOVELLO, EWER & CO.

NOVELLO, EWER & CO.'S
MUSIC PRIMERS
EDITED BY
SIR JOHN STAINER.

Any of the above may be had strongly bound in boards, price 6d. each extra.

LONDON & NEW YORK: NOVELLO, EWER AND CO.

Lightning Source UK Ltd.
Milton Keynes UK
UKHW041431260123
416012UK00004B/258